WIDER ASPECTS
OF EDUCATION

WIDER ASPECTS
OF EDUCATION

BY

J. HOWARD WHITEHOUSE & G. P. GOOCH

WITH AN INTRODUCTION BY

H. W. NEVINSON

CAMBRIDGE

AT THE UNIVERSITY PRESS

1924

CAMBRIDGE
UNIVERSITY PRESS

University Printing House, Cambridge CB2 8BS, United Kingdom

Published in the United States of America by Cambridge University Press, New York

Cambridge University Press is part of the University of Cambridge.

It furthers the University's mission by disseminating knowledge in the pursuit of education, learning and research at the highest international levels of excellence.

www.cambridge.org
Information on this title: www.cambridge.org/9781107625594

© Cambridge University Press 1924

First published 1924
First paperback edition 2013

A catalogue record for this publication is available from the British Library

ISBN 978-1-107-62559-4 Paperback

INTRODUCTION

BY H. W. NEVINSON

INTERNATIONAL Education I should call International Knowledge. It is one of the few hopeful things in human nature that if you get to know people you generally also get to like them. I remember at Oxford there was a very learned don who knew all about the society of ancient Athens rather more than two thousand years ago, but if you spoke to him about modern life, his only remark was, "I hate the lower classes." If you asked him further what he meant by the lower classes, he said, "I hate the working classes." It was only a case of ignorance. He had never spoken to a working man in his life except, perhaps, a plumber who, though inevitable as death, is not a good example. Consequently he knew nothing whatever about the working classes. Being a good-hearted man I am sure if he had known them he would not have expressed himself in that way. My favourite of all authors, my favourite character in all literature, Jonathan Swift, had a saying which exactly illustrates what I mean. He wrote to Pope, "I hate mankind, but I dearly love Tom,

John and Susan," or words to that purpose, showing that when he got to know individuals among mankind, his opinion of mankind in the lump began to alter.

I have heard people talk with horror about population, the appalling statistics of population, how population ought to be reduced, how this enormous mass of people, which they seem to regard as an ever increasing mouth, devouring the provisions of the world, must be a great disaster for the whole human race. Yet, if you bring one of these people face to face with a living baby—which is the population—he does not at once desire to kill it. It is a case of knowledge coming in, personal knowledge.

It is exactly like that with nations. Those of you who have studied the history of England a hundred years ago or rather more, at the time of the great wars against France, which lasted about twenty years, will know that the English people detested the French. Our great national hero, Nelson, writes in one of his letters, "The very name of Frenchman makes my blood boil. My first rule to my midshipmen is that they shall hate every Frenchman, whether Royalist, Republican, or nothing at all, they shall hate every Frenchman as they hate the devil" (quoted from memory). That was during war time. It was a case of ignorance. Since then we have come to know the French better. Perhaps we do not altogether agree with them or understand them, but if Nelson two or three years ago had said "The very name of Frenchman makes my blood boil," he would have got six months.

So it was with regard to our late enemies. During the war a report was spread that they were collecting the corpses of their own men and boiling them down into glycerine to make explosives for the guns. People believed that. It was a mere mistake in translation—ignorance of language in that case. They had taken the word meaning the carcase of an animal as though it meant the corpse of a human being. It showed a profound ignorance of the nature of the German people. An enormous number of people in England actually swallowed that abominable statement through ignorance, because they had probably never read a German book, and almost certainly had never been to Germany and become acquainted with the German people. These are instances of what I mean by a want of international education.

I do not myself believe that any country but one's own can be our spiritual home, because there is something deep and almost instinctive in the long bringing-up of childhood, in the intimacy of language—for however well you may speak another language, you never get it exactly the same as it is to the native—so many associations gather round every word, long associations of childhood, got from your nurse or your mother or the people in the street. You never can really enter into the language of any other country to perfection as you may into your own. Then there is also the long habit, the long tradition, the way of living, the way of thought, literature, religion, religious services, the look of the streets, even the smell of the towns, for each great city has a separate smell. All these things really make a native country, a spiritual home, and I do not think it is possible to have more than one spiritual home.

But we ought to remember that in our Father's house, which is this world, are many mansions, many abiding places, and you can become acquainted with those mansions by reading, by conversation, by travel—above all by travel—and by mixing freely with foreigners and not regarding them as our natural and national enemies.

To my mind this international education is far more sure of success in bringing peace to this world, which is the one thing we all desire, than even a League of Nations. In fact without this a League of Nations may become the mere mechanical instrument of diplomatists.

These few and random remarks were first

made by me at the Conference of Educational Associations to introduce the discussion of the subject by Mr Howard Whitehouse, whom we all know as one of our leading educationists both in theory and practice, and I commend the experiments for which he is responsible, which he describes in this book, to the consideration of all interested in education. I am glad that the book also contains two of the thoughtful and scholarly addresses delivered before the same conference by Dr Gooch.

NOTE

THE contents of this book were origin-
ally delivered as addresses. They are
published substantially in the form in
which they were given and no attempt has
been made to alter their colloquial character.

J. H. W.
G. P. G.

CONTENTS

CHAPTER ONE

THE TEACHING OF HISTORY IN RELATION TO
WORLD CITIZENSHIP : BY G. P. GOOCH, Litt.D.

IN speaking about citizenship in the year 1923, we must speak about world citizenship, and as a student and teacher of history I want this afternoon to try to suggest to you that the League of Nations is the consummation of the whole historic process; that it is a great deal more than a mere expedient rendered necessary by the Great War; indeed, that it is the logical, the natural and the rightful stage of the long process through which the human race has passed in attempting to organise the common life of man.

The key to the study of history is the unity of civilisation, and the key to the conception of world citizenship is also the unity of civilisation. Those of you who are teachers of history will, I am sure, be true to the principles of scholarship and also be true to the principles and demands of citizenship in its modern form by concentrating the attention of your pupils on this great conception of the unity of man. Civilisation is a co-operative achievement. The civilisation which we praise so highly is the result of the co-operative efforts of men and women, known and unknown, through all the ages, belonging to all countries and all races and all creeds. It is the most wonderful thing that the world has ever seen, and it is the result of the common efforts of the human family. I do not think any history teacher is worth his salt unless he has that occupying the background of his mind. If you teach English history you know, and you must make your pupils realise, that you are only teaching a small part of the great story of the life of humanity.

This conception of the unity of civilisation is not a very old conception nor a very new one. The founders of civilisation, in the sense in which we use it to-day, were the Greeks, but they had no conception of the unity of the human family. They knew nothing about the civilisations which had preceded their own, and they did not know and did not want to know anything about the civilisations by which they were surrounded. You know that the word *barbarians* was a Greek word to express people whose language sounded like *bar-bar* and was unintelligible to the cultured Athenian. The first glimmering of a perception of the unity of civilisation came in with the Roman Empire. The Romans, in addition to launching into the world the conception of law, also brought into the world the conception at any rate in an incipient form of the unity of civilised mankind, and by their conception of the law of nature and the law of nations they laid the foundation for the mental processes which we use to-day.

We know very well that the Roman Church was the heir—the spiritual if not the temporal heir—of the Roman Empire, and the Middle Ages are to me more interesting for their contributions to what we will call a political theory than for almost any other reason. For a thousand years, roughly from St Augustine to Machiavelli, from the fifth century to the fifteenth, the conception of the unity of civilisation dominated Europe. They called Europe the *Res publica Christiana*, the Christian Commonwealth; and they regarded every member of the Christian Commonwealth as a member of a single family. The head of that family—the unseen, invisible head—was God, who was represented on earth by two great potentates, the Emperor, who was supreme in secular matters, and the Pope, who was supreme in spiritual matters.

There was no such thing as what we call nowadays sovereignty. It never occurred to anybody that the prince or the ruler of any given State was supreme. It never occurred to anybody in the Middle Ages that any one country was responsible for its doings to itself alone. The

Middle Ages, I repeat, created and believed in this great conception of the unity of civilised mankind.

You will say, and say truly, that the conception was too narrow; that it was confined to Europe, and did not even embrace the whole of Europe because it excluded the Greek Church in the East; and that it was based on the community of religious belief instead of the common moral and spiritual foundations of human nature. Those objections are perfectly true, but they do not touch the value of this great contribution of medieval thought to the higher life of the world. They do not touch the value of the belief that mankind was one, and that every member and every State had recognised and confessed duties and obligations to all other States and to the community of which each State formed merely a part.

The difference between the medieval and the modern historian is immense. Modern historians, with few exceptions, are not only natives of their particular countries, but advocates. They are far less teachers and observers than advocates of a particular claim or a particular cause; and you can have—and do have—historians of the very front rank utterly ignorant of the underlying unity of civilised mankind. If you turn up any of the half-dozen historical hand-books which were read all over Christendom in the Middle Ages, you will find that the historian, as a matter of course, starts from the assumption of the unity of the Christian Commonwealth, and that he regards Christendom as a whole.

I come here this afternoon to try to plead for the restoration of the medieval conception of the unity of civilisation, brought up to date, secularised and informed with a new and a wider outlook. I also want you to realise that that conception of world citizenship—for such it was—which dominated Europe, or at any rate the better mind of Europe, for a thousand years, was lost under the double impact of the Renaissance and the Reformation: the Renaissance, which secularised thought and overthrew the spell of authority; and the Reformation, which broke the religious life of Christendom into two parts. For the last four centuries we have lived in an atmosphere from which the conception of world citizenship has almost entirely disappeared, to the unspeakable loss of the modern world.

About four hundred years ago, dating roughly from Machiavelli, the conception of sovereignty came into the modern world—the conception that every State was supreme, responsible only to itself, without any obligations to other States, without any obligations to the community of mankind, and without paying any more than lip homage either to a divine ruler of mankind or to the divine voice within. This doctrine of the unfettered sovereignty of the individual State has in my opinion been the curse of the modern world. It has been bad for civilisation as a whole, and it has been degrading for every State where it has been adopted. It is not the invention and has not been the property of any one country. I have traced it to Machiavelli, because Machiavelli was the first and remains to this day one of the most powerful political thinkers who ever lived; and his great achievement—his great and baneful achievement—was to divorce politics from ethics. What Machiavelli began was continued by men like Hobbes in England and Hegel in Germany, and has become something like an established commonplace of statesmen and of publicists in every country in the world. If any doctrine has ever been decisively condemned by the experience of its results, it has been the doctrine of the unfettered sovereignty of the individual State, which carried with it the denial of the conception of world citizenship.

For the last four centuries there has been a struggle going on for the soul of man between the doctrine of world citizenship, which was at any rate adumbrated in the Middle Ages, and the newer doctrine of purely secular and national politics. This struggle has mirrored itself not only in the acts of rulers and politicians, but also in the writings and the ideals of publicists. I am afraid we must say that the conception of world citizenship was the creed of a very tiny minority from the end of the fifteenth century to the beginning of the twentieth; but all the time there were men who looked back to the days when Europe was spiritually united and looked forward to the time when Europe, and indeed the world, might once again be spiritually united on the broader basis of a common humanity and on the broader basis of the obligations which every member of the human family feels and ought to feel to every other.

And this process, this antagonism, has now led us to a period where I think the tide has at last begun to turn. I regard the Great War as the inevitable result and the final disproof of the truth and value of narrow-hearted and narrow-minded nationalism, and I believe that the best thought and the best mind of the day in all countries without exception is turning back to the medieval conception of world citizenship, brought up to date, transferred from a theological to an ethical foundation, and enlarged until it embraces at any rate all the civilised countries of the world. This process has been assisted not only by the bankruptcy of the old doctrine of sovereignty which was revealed in the Great War, but also by our experience of the results of the struggle.

One of the tasks of the historian is to realise that his duty is to inquire into and to explain the whole life of humanity. As I am addressing some teachers, I should like to point out that it is impossible to deal with the history of any one country in isolation from the main stream of human development. As we are English people, and as we teach more English history than any other history, just let me remind you that it is quite impossible to teach English history faithfully, clearly or wisely without keeping continually in mind the fact that it is only a portion of a very much larger story. What are the most fundamental elements in our national life and in the nationality of every modern State? The first is race, the second is language, and the third is religion.

If you take what we call the British race, it is mixed to a degree which it requires an effort to realise. The first racial element which we can trace in our land is what we call the Iberian, which connects us with the early civilisation of Spain and North Africa; the second element was the British; and the third was the Roman. But there was no such thing as Roman blood.

The blood that was brought into Britain and mixed with British blood during the four centuries of the Roman occupation was Roman only in name, because the Roman administrators and the Roman garrisons were drawn from every part of the known world—from Europe, from Northern Africa and from Western Asia. They all came to Britain, and large numbers of them married and left traces of their blood here. After the Romans we had two great series of Teutonic invasions, and after that we had the infiltration of the Norman blood, which had been enriched by long residence in the North of France but which retained the vigour of its northern ancestors.

Since then we have had at intervals most valuable contributions to the common stock of what we call English or British blood, from the Flemings, the Huguenots, and in the nineteenth century from almost every nation under heaven. Therefore our blood, which is the most fundamental thing in our life, mutely speaks to us of world citizenship, and tells us that we are part of the great human family.

In a slightly lesser degree our language teaches us the same truth. Our language is not a Teutonic language, as some people used to say and as some people still appear to think. It is a mixture. The basis is Teutonic, but the superstructure is Latin. The short words, roughly speaking, are Teutonic, and come from the North of Europe; and the longer words are, roughly speaking, Latin, and come from the South of Europe. During the nineteenth century we have added a third and very important element to our language, namely, the Greek element. As we have advanced we have found it necessary to go back to ancient Greece to express abstract thoughts and to invent names for certain branches of study. The number of Greek words that we use in the course of the day, if we are talking about the higher branches of education or culture, is very numerous. If you take words like *logic*, *metaphysics*, *political economy*, *psychology*, *pathology*, or many others which are constantly on our lips, you will find that they all come from Greece. Therefore we have got at any rate three quite distinct foreign elements in our speech: the Teutonic, which comes from North Europe; the Latin, which comes from Rome, partly direct and partly through France; and finally, in later times, this small but extremely important infiltration from the Greek language. So I say that the language which we speak to-day is a composite achievement, and every word of every sentence we utter reminds us that we are citizens of the world, that we are simply one member of the great human family, and that it is above all our connection with that human family which has made us what we are.

It is exactly the same with religion. Our religion is a foreign import. We had religion before the coming of St Augustine, but there was not very much left of what we had in those days, and ever since 600 A.D. we have formed part of the great Christian family. We were converted by a missionary sent from Rome. But Christianity did not begin in Rome; it began in Palestine. The Christian religion which was preached in Palestine was not founded there *ab initio* or *ab ovo*. It was, like all other great influences and movements in the world, itself a very composite affair. The relations between Christianity and Judaism are in many directions very close, and we must trace back Christianity, or part of it, not only to the Jews but to the Babylonians, from whom the Jews got so many of their ideas; and we must trace it back, not only to the Babylonians but to the people who lived in the Mesopotamian Plains before even the Babylonians, those mysterious Sumerians who are now coming into their own. We get also the later influences of that great mass of competing religions and philosophical ideas, with which the Roman Empire was fermenting at the time of the life of Christ and the life of

St Paul and the fathers and systematisers of Christian dogma. Therefore you will see that the Christian religion, which is the religion of our country and has been for thirteen hundred years, makes us feel, if we know where it came from, that we are connected not only with the life of Continental Europe, but even with the remoter ages and the development of the religious consciousness not only in Europe but in the nearer part of Asia.

I have called attention to these fundamental factors in our life in order to try to give teachers a certain concrete feeling, which they may be able to pass on to their pupils, that we are really citizens of the world in our blood, in our speech, and in the religion of our country.

But you can pass on to other things which will teach you the same lesson. Our literature for one. English literature, unless it had been fertilised by French and Italian influences— without going further afield than those two great sources of inspiration and enrichment—would have been a very poor affair. Take our art. Look at our Norman and then at our Gothic cathedrals. Their very names tell us and remind us that we owe them to foreign influences. The architecture which has dominated this country for nearly four hundred years, which we call Italian or Renaissance, in its turn teaches the same lesson

—that we have got to look for its origins to Italy, and through Italy to the ancient world.

I have tried to explain that what we may call the fundamental factors of our life connect us with the main stream of human development. I should like very rapidly, just in order to illustrate my thesis, to remind you that a teacher of a course of English history can never explain how we have developed and how we have become what we are without constant reference to our connection and contact with the wider life and the main stream of European civilisation. What we call civilisation in this country in the modern sense begins with the coming of the Romans. For four centuries we were part of the Roman Empire—an elementary fact, but a fact which is hardly realised by the majority of teachers, which is systematically neglected in the majority of text-books, and which is forgotten to a degree which surprises me. The first great influence which helped to build up civilisation in this country was the fact that we were for four hundred years part of the Roman Empire. The next great influence which helped to build up our civilisation was the coming of the Teutons from North Europe in a series of waves, bringing in the conception of personal and political liberty, which is one of the most precious and one of the most enduring elements in our national character.

The third great influence which helped to build up our English civilisation was the fact that we became part of the Medieval Church. It began with the coming of Augustine; but it was not until the Norman Conquest that we became still more intimately attached to the life of the Medieval Church both as an institution and as a teacher. In old days it was part of the Protestant tradition that England was never what we may call a full member of the Catholic family of nations. We were referred to the Statute of Præmunire to suggest that we had got only one leg in the Roman camp. That is quite incorrect. One of the many things that the great legal historian Professor Maitland achieved, was to show that the Canon law which was used in our country was exactly the same as that which was used elsewhere, and we now know that right up to the Reformation England was part and parcel of the Roman system. Though that produced a number of results which were sharply resented, sometimes by the kings and sometimes by the people of our country, there is not the slightest doubt that our connection with what was then the most civilising influence in the world, was of incalculable advantage to our own race and to the building up of our civilisation.

The fourth great influence which helped to

build up the civilisation which we describe as English, was the Norman Conquest. The Norman Conquest involved the attachment of England to a certain part of Western Europe for about a hundred and fifty years, and it brought with it some of the disabilities which always attach to government by a foreign dynasty. But it came to an end, and, looking back on it, I think we shall feel that the Norman Conquest enriched and enlarged our national outlook to an incalculable degree.

The next great influence after the Norman Conquest, the fifth I am going to mention, was the Reformation. Although the Reformation cut us off from Rome, to whom we owed so much, it compensated for that by increasing the closeness of our contact with North or Protestant Europe, and as a matter of fact it governed our foreign policy for the next couple of centuries. The policy of Elizabeth, of Cromwell and of William III, was really based upon the fact that we had become a Protestant nation, and that as a Protestant nation we felt bound to throw in our lot with other Protestant nations in the North of Europe to prevent the Catholic counter-revolution from regaining the territories which it had lost.

I have briefly sketched what I regard as the main formative influences of our own island story—the Roman rule, the coming of the Teutons, our inclusion in the family of the Roman Church and the belief of the Roman Church, the Norman Conquest and the Reformation—every one of them on the one hand enriching our national life and character and culture, and on the other hand linking us by ever fresh bonds and contacts to the wider life of mankind.

When you come to our own modern centuries you find the contacts getting so numerous that it is almost impossible to enumerate them. One of the greatest unifiers of the modern world has been science—not only scientific inventions but also scientific ideas—and one of the great achievements of the last three or four centuries has been the growing unification of what we may call the higher thought and the higher culture of the world. During the eighteenth, and in an increasing degree during the nineteenth, century any ideas in the realm of philosophy and any discoveries in the realm of science immediately became the common property of mankind, and in every single case established a new telegraph wire between one country and every other. Such unifying influences as travel, and the invention of railways and steamships, and the internationalisation of finance, and the organisation of international conferences, whether for purposes of business or of study, each one of these things has helped to deepen the conviction of our world citizenship.

Finally—and this perhaps has been a more important influence on the man in the street than all the others I have mentioned—there has been the Great War, which made us feel that for good and evil we are all members of a single, even if of a very quarrelsome, human family.

I have selected a few concrete examples in order to prove and push home my deep conviction, that if you are going to understand and teach history properly, you must teach our national history as part of the general process. I should not like you to go away with the idea that I think everything of value in our national life and character has come from abroad. That would be going just as far in the other direction as the narrow insularity which thinks nothing of our debt to other nations. Civilisation, I repeat once more, is the result of the co-operative achievements of the great nations of the world, our own included and our own occupying one of the front seats. If I were to take French, German, Italian or Spanish history I should be able to give you an exactly similar illustration of the interconnection and interdependence of its development with the development of the wider life of mankind.

I hope I have said enough to convince you, as I have long been convinced myself, that to teach history effectively, and to study it and understand it thoroughly, it must be studied as a whole. When we have that formula lodged in our mind, and when we have it proved and illustrated by a thousand proofs and illustrations—and I have only given you a few this afternoon—then it seems to me that you have the strongest and surest foundation for the practical tasks of citizenship as they present themselves to us at the opening of the twentieth century.

This League of Nations idea is not very old and not very new. A year or two ago a learned Dutch professor published a long and erudite volume, tracing back the idea of an association of nations into the Middle Ages and summarising no less than twenty-nine distinct systems for an association of nations between the fourteenth century and the end of the eighteenth. There is no need to go through this list. It is enough for our purpose to-day to remind you that just because in the sixteenth century the old idea of the Christian Commonwealth was dead and the newer doctrine of national sovereignty was very much alive, some of the wisest men in all countries saw that it was wrong and began to plan out schemes for peaceful co-operation between the nations of the world. Every great war brought a new system. The continual civil and foreign wars of Henry IV of France inspired in him the Great Design—*le grand dessein*—which was the first detailed scheme for keeping the peace which had been put forward by any man of wide celebrity.

It was the Thirty Years' War which inspired Grotius to lay the foundations of international law, and international law, as I need hardly remind you, trusts to moral sanctions and not to physical sanctions to enforce its awards. The appeal to moral sanctions, which was made by Grotius, would have no sense unless he believed, as he did believe, that each nation was only one member of a common family. The wars against France at the end of the seventeenth century inspired William Penn, our glorious old English Quaker, to his wonderful little tract on "Perpetual Peace," which is a very close anticipation of the Covenant of 1919. The long Marlborough wars inspired the Abbé St Pierre, who was one of France's plenipotentiaries at the Congress of Utrecht, to write the most elaborate and detailed scheme of an association of nations which saw the light until the Covenant of the League of Nations was produced in the year 1919. It was the War arising from the French Revolution which inspired Immanuel Kant to his magnificent little tract on "Perpetual Peace," in which he asked not only for an association of nations, but for an association of self-governing nations, thereby linking up the conception of peace with the conception of democratic self-government. It was the terrible struggle against Napoleon which inspired the Tsar, Alexander of Russia, to his project of an alliance of nations, which he worked out in the year 1805, ten years before the Holy Alliance was brought into existence.

Those few names, some of thinkers and some of rulers, and all of different nationalities, will serve to remind you of the fact that some of the wisest men of the modern world felt uncomfortable and unhappy breathing an atmosphere of unlimited national sovereignty.

During the nineteenth century, curiously enough, the stream flowed underground. There was not one single thinker during the nineteenth century of any note who put forward the idea of a League of Nations as a means of keeping the peace and saving the nations from eating each other up. The forward-looking thinkers of the nineteenth century turned to arbitration. Arbitration produced some useful results, but the hopes on which it was founded proved in the long run to be disappointing. Too much was asked of it. Arbitration is only of real and decisive importance when the elements which go to the making of wars are not too strong for its application; and all the elements that go to the making of wars were piling up during the nineteenth century. The new sentiment of nationality was one; the balance of power was another; the exploitation of Africa and Asia was a third. All these things were making an electric atmosphere which was far too dangerous for the comparatively mild instrument of arbitration to deal with, and therefore when the Great War broke out in 1914, people began by common accord to see that arbitration was not enough and that we wanted a fundamental overhauling of international relationships. We wanted the creation of a new machinery for international intercourse, but we wanted something much better than that—we wanted the scrapping and burial of the doctrine of unfettered national sovereignty, and we wanted the revival of the grand old medieval doctrine that we are all parts of the human family and that in consequence we all owe obligations to one another.

I think I have said enough to convince you that the unity of civilisation is the key, both to the teaching of history and to the performance of our new duties as citizens of the world. Most of us are old enough to remember the time when the words "citizens of the world" were a phrase of rhetoric which occurred occasionally in perorations and was occasionally laughed at by people who suggested that those who used it and those who claimed to be citizens of the world cared nothing about their own country. Now we know very well that not in a rhetorical sense, but in a political and juridical sense, we are all of us citizens of the world, because our country is one of the members of the Covenant of the League of Nations, and that that membership brings with it duties just as definite and just as important as our membership of the British Empire and our English citizenship. To me, as a student of history and as a keen supporter of the League of Nations, it is a great comfort to feel, as I do feel, that the study of the past and the needs of the present both point in the same direction, namely, to get a real, clear, close grip of this fundamental fact—that we are all members of the human family.

It will take a very long time for this conception to work itself into the consciousness and the subconsciousness of statesmen, of the man in the street, and of the schoolmaster, and of the author of school histories; but it has got to come, and it will come. I am perfectly certain that those of us who are connected with teaching and the teaching profession will be gravely neglecting our duties if we do not do all that lies in our power first to convince ourselves of this fundamental fact of the unity of civilisation and the mutual obligation of all the members of the civilised family of man; and, in the second place, if we do not do all that we can to pass on this great revealing and inspiring conception to those with whom we come in contact and to those whose training is given into our hands.

CHAPTER TWO

EDUCATIONAL CO-OPERATION WITH AMERICA : BY G. P. GOOCH, Litt.D.

SINCE the Washington Conference, the United States and ourselves have created —and I hope will maintain—a new intimacy, which is already beginning to bear fruit, and which, if continued, as I believe it will and ought to be, will be of incalculable blessing to the whole of the civilised world.

I am not going to ask for a more systematic study of American literature, because it seems to me that on the whole English people have given sufficient study to American literature. I do not say that in a disparaging way of American literature. I say it by way of praise of the British reader. The contrast between our careful study of American literature and our almost studied and systematic neglect of American history and institutions is very extraordinary. American literature is not very great in bulk, but much of it is very high in quality. We have a large number of books on individual American writers. Men like Emerson, Lowell, Whittier, and Longfellow have been studied at least as reverently and as appreciatively, and perhaps I may add as critically, in our country as in America. One of the latest publications of my own university of Cambridge is that excellent encyclopædic survey, the *Cambridge History of American Literature*.

When I pass to American history, I repeat that I find the most extraordinary contrast. My place at this table is going to be taken at four o'clock by my friend, Mr Laski, and I have got on my notes a sentence from the preface to his last volume of essays. This is what Mr Laski says: "The study of American history and politics has barely been attempted in Great Britain." That is a very extraordinary thing to say in the year 1921, but it happens to be only too true. There are extraordinarily few books written by English writers about American history and American institutions. I expect it has occurred to you all that in that famous *vade mecum* of the cultured man and woman, Macaulay's *Essays*, not one is devoted to America. A few years ago a most excellent little study, a mere outline history of America, was published by that remarkable man Goldwin Smith. To this day that outline is about the best brief bird's-eye view of the development of America. Perhaps it is a little humiliating if I add that he only wrote the book after he had shaken the dust of Oxford and England off his feet and had gone to the more bracing atmosphere of Canada.

The best work done on American history by British writers has been devoted to the Colonial period, and we think above all of those massive works of Payne and Doyle. Only one British historian of the first rank has ever given serious study to American history; but there again, I hasten to add that Lecky did not look round for a subject and deliberately put his hand upon America. He determined to write a history of England and Ireland in the eighteenth century, and in the pursuit of his task he naturally came to the American War of Independence, and took it in his stride. But I am bound to say in his praise that his chapters on the American War of Independence and on the dispute between George III and the American colonies are one of the glories of British scholarship.

Another author of quite different character has written a very delightful book on the American Revolution—Sir George Trevelyan. Sir George began his literary life by a fascinating book on the early life of Charles James Fox, and in later life—after he had retired from his long and somewhat stormy political career—he took up the theme where he had left off and continued Fox's life until it broadened out into a survey of the American War. You will find that book romantic, pictorial, scintillating with that literary charm which he inherited from his uncle, Macaulay, and which he has handed on to his own son, the biographer of Bright, Garibaldi, and Lord Grey. But his book on the American War of Independence belongs, if I may say so without offence, perhaps rather to the literary than to the scientific department of history.

You will ask me, perhaps, to recommend you at any rate one really good book written in English and published in England on American history. For advanced readers there is nothing to compare with the seventh volume of the *Cambridge Modern History*, which is entirely devoted to the United States, and contains contributions by British and American scholars. It begins long before the United States ceased to be colonies, and it comes right down to our own time. If that volume had been published separately, it would probably have sold more and been more read and studied. Before I pass away from the first portion of my address, namely, British scholarship on America, I must naturally refer to the great work of Lord Bryce. It is above all a study of living, modern America. But great, memorable, and exhaustive as that book is, do not let us forget that in a certain sense it is unintelligible without a fairly careful study of the earlier history of the great nation to which he has devoted so much time and care and thought.

I think we have reached the position that the amount of British attention devoted to America is extraordinarily small. One or two really good books, like those of Bryce and Lecky, a scholarly essay on the American Constitution by Sir Henry Maine, and one or two good surveys of the Colonial period, are an astonishingly small harvest when you compare the work of our British historical scholars on America with their work on almost any of the other Great Powers of Europe. Here is an almost virgin field. I am glad to have this opportunity of expressing my conviction that it is a subject which well repays attention. Quite apart from its political interest, its historical and philosophical value is of the highest quality.

If we are to learn much about American history and institutions, you will have gathered from my brief, and perhaps a little disparaging, account of British scholarship that we must go to American writers. Here the first thing that strikes one is something not altogether creditable to ourselves. We do not neglect American historians. The most celebrated American historians have nowhere had more numerous and appreciative readers. Where was Washington

Irving more read and enjoyed, or Prescott, or Mahan's interpretation of the naval history of Modern Europe? Where, I might say, going to a somewhat deeper and more specialised field, was the superb and massive scholarship of America's greatest medievalist, Henry Charles Lea, more admired than among medievalists in England? But, without exception, these men were writing about a country which was not their own. So we reach this curious paradox, that we English people, broadly speaking, only read American historians when they are not writing about their own country. There are reasons for that as for everything. One is that most of the men I have mentioned happened to be extraordinarily gifted writers. Another is that there is a deep, I might almost say an ineradicable, conviction in the British mind that American history is dull.

I have to leave these brilliant American historians, because they have not been writing about their own country, and I want to suggest to you one or two reasons why you should at any rate attempt to cultivate an interest in American history and institutions. I think you may take my word for it, that if you make the attempt you will succeed. If you can once break through what you may call the uninviting crust of American history and get inside, you will be astonished at its wealth of personal, political, and, in the highest sense of the word, philosophical interest.

We have a sort of unspoken conviction that when America became independent, she did not concern us any more. We know far more about the Colonial period than about the period of independence. But when you get past the story of the early Puritan and Quaker settlements in the seventeenth century, there is nothing in the Colonial years to compare in interest with the period which sets in with the Declaration of Independence.

There have been two epochs in the history of independent America, in which you get the two things necessary to produce a really satisfying historical subject—great happenings and a ferment of ideas. You can have great happenings without much ferment of ideas, but when you find them both—as you do in the Reformation, as you do in the time of our Puritan Commonwealth, as you do in the French Revolution, as you do in the period of the making of the American Constitution, and in the slavery discussion of the middle of the nineteenth century —you have subjects which not only appeal to our craving for personality, for colour, for the ebb and flow of great events, but involve the necessity of considering the motives and the great ideals which inspired the parties and the armies which met and clashed.

I would like to say a word or two about these two great periods of American history: the foundation of the Constitution and the Slavery struggle. It is extraordinary how little we know, and how little we care to know, about the early years of the United States. We know that Washington was a great general, but how many English people know anything about his Presidency? How many English people have ever read a book about Washington? If anybody here has got the power of writing a book about Washington, comparable in interest and in popular appeal to Lord Charnwood's *Abraham Lincoln*, I beg him to set about it without undue delay. How many English people know about that extraordinarily interesting man—one of the most consistent and true-hearted democrats who ever lived—Jefferson; a man who connected the Old World with the New; an American Rousseau; a man who took back from France all the generous ideas with which the mind of the eighteenth century was fermenting? How many people in England know about that extraordinary dynasty—because you can call it nothing else—the dynasty of the house of Adams? John Adams, the President; John Quincy Adams, his son, a second President;

Charles Francis Adams, the grandson, the
American Ambassador during the Civil War;
and the sons of the Ambassador, Henry and
Charles, who have also played a great part in
modern American history in diplomacy and
scholarship. If a dynasty of that character had
existed anywhere except in America, we should
know all about it.

The only exception to our stolid ignorance
of the great creative period of American history
—when the Constitution was being beaten out,
when the parties were forming, when the great
strife was going on between the Federalists and
the Democrats, the forerunners of the central-
isers and the decentralisers—is Alexander
Hamilton. We are fortunate in having two
books on him which have been much read
—Mr Oliver's brilliant *Essay* and Gertrude
Atherton's extraordinarily accurate historical
novel called *The Conqueror*. There is as much
history in it as fiction, in fact, a great deal more.
If you read it you will carry with you to the
end of your days a living picture of the most
brilliant figure in American history. Before I
leave the early period I must just say also that it
is a disaster that there is no good book on
Benjamin Franklin. You can buy—and I hope
most of you have bought and read—his *Auto-
biography*, but it does not go very far. Its main

value is to interest you in the man who, in later life, became one of the creators of America.

If we know little of the founders, we at any rate know their names; but many educated Englishmen do not know even the names of the great protagonists in the slavery struggle. I am sure I need not remind anyone here that the Civil War was simply the fifth act of the great drama which had been developing for several decades. The battles were simply the material solution of the conflict of ideas which had raged in parliaments, in the press, in the world of fiction, in society, and in men's souls and consciences for a generation.

When the old generation of Empire makers died out—and Jefferson was the last of them—a dense bank of fog descends on the English mind as regards America, and the whole of American history is wrapt in gloom until Abraham Lincoln reaches the White House and the guns go off at Fort Sumter. Yet in those thirty or forty years, say from 1820 to 1860, you will find a subject of extraordinary interest. You have the clash not only of ideals but of theories and principles, and you will see brilliant presentations and representatives of opposing ideas. We always think of the struggle of North and South as a struggle about slavery. That was the way it appeared to people like Garrison and the author of *Uncle Tom's Cabin*; but to the man in the street and the statesman it was as a problem of centralisation or decentralisation, between the sovereign power of the Federal Government and the traditional freedom of the separate States. It was the old struggle as to where sovereignty resided. If you believe, like Hobbes, that you must place all your sovereignty under one hat, it is very simple; indeed, too simple. But if you do not believe that sovereignty can be fixed and rounded off and pent in, if you believe that it is diffused, you are up against the difficult problem as to what has become of it. Thus the question of slavery loomed up as a matter of sovereignty.

The two great names in this battle of theory are Daniel Webster, the champion of the centralists, and Calhoun, the champion of State rights. These two men fought one another in speech and in pamphlet for a long course of years. They both died something like ten years before the problem—which they found it impossible to solve or to compromise upon—was fought out on the battlefield. One of the main causes of interest in this controversy is the novelty of the issue, due to the fact that we have never had Federal Government in our own country, and thus avoided the problem of where we are to draw the line of self-determination.

We are a unitary State, and in a unitary State at any rate it is not so difficult—although I will not say it is very easy—to locate sovereignty. Over here we say that sovereignty resides in the King and Parliament, though it may equally well be argued that it resides in the electorate. But when you get a Federal Government, as in America, and the provincial and particularist traditions of the Colonies, most of them far more than a hundred years old before the Central Government even came into existence at Washington, you will readily understand that the location of sovereignty, the question whether the State had a right to secede if it objected to something that the Central Government did or did not do, was a new issue. I venture to say that no student of political theory ought to go very far in his studies without considering the great debate on State rights, of which slavery was only an illustration. Although that issue was settled by the sword, it was simply one form of the problem that we have still confronting us, a problem which has never been more topical than since the great watchword of self-determination was flung into a fermenting world by President Wilson.

When Lincoln comes on the scene, interest in England in American history begins to revive. Our fathers and grandfathers were all interested in the Civil War—some for commercial reasons, others for broader and more human reasons— and in the radiant figure of Lincoln, whose greatness was only realised in this country after he had gone, who was infinitely more human than any of the founders of the American Constitution, and was infinitely more lovable than Washington. The mere fact that he was a great human being did much to rekindle English interest in American history and institutions.

In our own time, when the world has become one, and, above all, since the Spanish-American War, British interest in American history and institutions has been increasing. Modern American politics will become more real to us if we read Thayer's life of that splendid man— one of the best men America ever produced— John Hay, and the official life of Roosevelt by his old friend Bishop.

The best way of achieving educational co-operation with America, apart from the interchange of students and professors, is for them to know more about us and for us to know more about them as they are to-day, and more about the way in which they have grown to be what they are to-day. You cannot understand modern politics unless you know the roots from which they grew. People have acted as they did mainly because they thought as they did.

You can never understand happenings unless you get behind them, unless you get back to intellectual and spiritual forces, to emotional instincts and ideals. It would be of educational, no less than political, value if more time and attention were given in our schools and universities to the problems of American history and institutions. After all there is such a thing as the Anglo-Saxon tradition. I do not desire a political alliance with America or any other country. In a world in which a League of Nations exists there is no need, and I should say no justification, for alliances. But you can have a subtler sort of alliance; you can have the instinctive understanding which comes from the inheritance of great and uplifting traditions. The closer we approach to one another, the more we realise both the resemblances and the differences in our outlook and in our history, the greater will be our power to maintain the best elements—and many of them are very noble—of the Anglo-Saxon tradition.

CHAPTER THREE

AMERICAN EXPERIMENTS IN EDUCA-
TION : BY J. HOWARD WHITEHOUSE

T HERE is a wholly different system of education in America from that which exists
here. Put briefly, the system of popular education in this country is a *class* system. The term
elementary education does not mean the education we consider suitable for children of a certain
age. Secondary education does not mean the
kind of education we consider suitable for
children of a certain age. Elementary education
in this country means the education we consider
suitable for children of a certain social class, and,
roughly speaking, secondary education is the
system we consider most suitable for children
of another social class.

The United States of America comprise about
fifty States, many of them larger than this
country, and each self-governing as far as its
educational system is concerned. Practically in
each one of these States there is the same kind
of popular education. Elementary education
there means the education appropriate to a
certain age. Secondary education and university
education mean, again, the education appropriate

to certain ages. The terms have no relation whatever to any class system. The elementary school is free, with all its books and apparatus; the students passing naturally on to the secondary school, and these schools again are wholly free both as regards tuition, books, and equipment; and, in a large number of States, high school pupils may pass on to a university which is similarly free. America realises that her best policy is to cultivate the brains of her citizens, and she does not consider that the brains of her citizens are confined to any one social class. I hope that what I am saying does not sound violently revolutionary!

Now, I will try to give you in a word or two a picture of the arrangements in connection with elementary schools and secondary schools in the United States. I will not take New York as a typical American city, though I shall have something to say about its educational system, because New York is not a typical American city, but I will take an elementary school as it exists in hundreds of typical American cities. They have, in the States, practically achieved the common school. These free State schools are so good that none can compete with them; there is no question of private competition; there is no question of vested interests, either in religion or school buildings. All these things

are unknown. If I may say so, people do not
waste their time, so far as education is concerned,
in idle quarrels. They concern themselves with
real problems of education. In typical towns
and cities throughout the United States the
common school has been created. You will find
in the form rooms practically all the children of
the town; the children of wealthy people sitting
side by side with children of the poorest people;
no one can fail to realise that it is a common
school. I am not standing here as an advocate
of any particular kind of school at this moment,
but to set forth facts, and I know that in this
country, when the common school has been
talked about as an ideal, many practical objections have been raised. One that has seemed
quite reasonable to me is this: how can you hope
for a common school here in London, or anywhere in England, where children come from
different households, with varying standards of
physical cleanliness, varying standards of habits
and so on? Now, I want to show you how that
difficulty is met in the common elementary
schools of America.

I put that criticism to the heads of these
schools, and one after the other showed me how
they met and overcame the difficulty. I well
remember—I am speaking now of an experience
I had in the city of Buffalo, but the same story

could be told of any other typical American town—the reply of the head of one of the elementary schools in that town, who said, "Let me show you how we deal with the question of physical cleanliness, and how, instead of its being a question of living down to the lowest standard, we make it a matter of living up to the highest." He took me to a magnificent dressing-room where every child, each morning, puts his clothes, each in his own wire compartment, with warm air sweeping through to dry and cleanse them.

From this great room a boy, having stripped, goes to another room where many shower baths are fitted, stands under a warm shower bath, and regards it as a privilege to be able to do so. I was surprised to see how complete was the scientific fitting up of these rooms, so that it is not possible for the hot water to splash from the body of one child on to the body of another. That is a detail, just to show the care that is taken in these matters. Having gone under the shower bath, the last of these acts of daily ritual takes place. The head took me into a room containing a magnificent swimming bath where every boy can swim or be taught to swim every morning for ten or fifteen minutes. I was not surprised to find that it was one of the most popular features of the daily life of the school, and that no boy ever

considered it any reflection on him to undergo
that ceremony.

It would probably be a surprise to each of us
to learn that no money is grudged on the cause
of education in America. I think I have sometimes heard rumours of criticism about the cost
of education in this country, and I have sometimes felt that the motives that inspire us
occasionally to be generous in this matter are
not always quite above criticism. If I may
mention such exalted names in public, I would
say that I was a little surprised myself, in a
recent debate in the House of Commons, to
learn on the authority of the Prime Minister
himself that the reason why you should pay
teachers in this country good wages—or begin
to do so—was because if they were not paid
good salaries they would preach dangerous
revolutionary doctrines. In America there is
what I might almost call competition in supplying
every possible need for the purpose of education.
No money appears to be grudged on school
buildings, school equipment, and upon giving
the teachers every possible facility for carrying
on their work under the best possible conditions. You have only to see these equipments
—swimming baths, shower baths, and practical
workrooms—attached to elementary schools to
realise how true this is. Indeed, it is only

natural that this should be so, because in America every one realises that the cause of education is something that concerns themselves and their children. No one there regards money spent on education as a form of extravagance to be severely repressed. I know no country in the world where more money in proportion to its population is spent on the cause of education.

I have given you a picture in connection with the progressive elementary schools in America. Let me now speak of the secondary schools, which again are quite free. Anyone who said in America to a gathering of experts in education that all children who were capable of profiting by further education should go to a secondary school would be laughed at, because, unless a child is only suited for a mental or physical hospital, they regard *every* child as suitable for further forms of instruction after it leaves the elementary school. They have no use for a ladder from the elementary to the secondary school; what they need is a broad highway. Therefore the children go in great numbers, and almost automatically, from the State elementary to the State secondary school. These secondary schools are fitted up—I am not at the moment talking of the principles of education, but of the machinery—in a most efficient way. So far as science can be applied to the things of the school, it is applied alike in the elementary and the secondary schools of America.

I would like to give you an idea of the arrangements in connection with the secondary schools in New York, which, in this respect, are typical except with regard to the size of the school. New York, being built on a tongue of land, has to be erected towards the heavens. I think I am right in saying that there is not a single secondary school in New York which has less than 5000 pupils. That is not because they believe in a school of 5000, but because the physical difficulties of living in New York are such that they are obliged to have schools containing that enormous number of children. I visited many secondary schools in New York, and found certain common features in them. There is a much greater variety in the curriculum, there are greater facilities than in this country for practical work. You have frequently your forge, your printing room, your casting room, and all kinds of rooms devoted to arts and crafts and technical processes. You find an equipment in some respects that you would look for in an up-to-date university. A secondary school of 5000 boys in New York is a picture of efficiency and organisation. So far as I could observe in frequent visits, the machinery of these boys' schools worked with great precision. You go

into a large interesting room which is covered
with a series of charts. You think, first of all,
that you have come into a room where an
attempt is being made to show the history of
the world in the form of charts on the walls;
but it is simply a list of the classes. The faculty
comprises over 250 persons, and the work of
the school is organised by subjects. There will
be an English department, a French department,
and so on. You are shown what can be done
by the application of science to a school, and by
no niggardliness in the spending of money. You
see a machinery which is as good as machinery
can be made. And the picture you get in New
York is repeated in other towns and cities
throughout America, but not on the same size,
because, happily, the same physical difficulties
do not exist in other cities on the same scale as
in New York.

If I had time I could tell you many details
about the secondary schools. I was interested
by a book which is issued every term and is
given to every boy or girl in the school. This
book contains about a hundred pages. It gives
a list of clubs and societies covering every form
of intellectual and physical activity; it gives
rules of health; information as to how to proceed
to your university; it gives a bibliography of
books on various subjects which are essential

to the student. It presents a picture of the working of this vast machinery of the school in the clearest way, and this book itself is a tribute to efficiency, revealing the extraordinary activities of the school. It is also written in very good, clear English.

Before coming to detailed experiments, I want to say something about the university system in the United States.

There are, I suppose, about 1000 universities in the United States. These universities are common universities in the sense that the schools are common schools, and, of course, they are used to a far greater extent than the universities are in this country. I should like to give you an account of my experience at one of the universities in America—the University of Syracuse. I was a guest of that university for some time, and had many opportunities of studying and informing myself with regard to its working by direct consultation with the faculty which is responsible for its government and all details in connection with it.

Syracuse is an unlovely town and offers no features of special interest, but the university, which stands on high ground on the borders of the city, is a singularly beautiful place. It has some hundreds of acres; it has a great amphitheatre for sports and games; it has a swimming bath, art galleries, and the equipment of a modern university. Its buildings and equipment are splendid. Yet I am speaking of something which is typical of hundreds of universities.

The question I put to the authorities was: How far is this university, with its splendid equipment, the university of the whole of the city? Do the poor come here? Or is it attended only by men of the middle or well-to-do classes? I asked, because it was not a wholly free university like the city of New York. I was assured by the professors, and by the governing body, that the poorest came, and that it was a university which contained every one; no one had been kept out by reason of poverty.

What I heard made me realise something of the love for learning which the educational system of America calls forth in the youth of the nation. The Professor of History said: "Let me give you an instance of the kind of spirit in the university and of the kind of students we get. I went down to-day to the town and left an order for my wife at the butcher's (for in America they speak of these things without any shame), where I thought I recognised the young man who took my order. I found he was one of the students in the history department, who spent two hours daily serving in the butcher's shop in order to get the necessary money to maintain himself at the university." The professor said further: "Many of our students today, in the long vacation, take posts as waiters, and even as trolley conductors, in order, during the vacation, to get money to pay for their university residence."

Another professor, speaking again before his colleagues without any embarrassment, said: "Let me now give you an instance. As a youth I was a member of this university. I paid my way through the university and graduated here by spending an hour or two each day removing the ashes and cleaning the garden paths of one of the professors of the university." And, he added, "This very day one of my students is removing my ashes and keeping my garden paths in order." I think we shall look in vain, in other places, for a parallel to such popular zeal for education. Yet the same story can be told of any other university in a typical American town.

The results of the common educational system of America are, in the first place, a united feeling with regard to education. We find it very difficult to convene a conference in this country at which educational leaders and representatives of education would have a common interest. Here there are public schools, private schools, council schools, continuation schools, and so on. We should also find it difficult to get education considered as a national system of our own, in which all are interested. In America the best brains of the country, so far as education is concerned, write and speak and think of education as the State popular system in which every one is interested. This has come from having a common system.

I will take, next, the general system of education in America, and I want to tell you of one or two experiments, which I think most suggestive and stimulating, and which will repay study in this country. I call them "experiments," but their success has already been demonstrated.

The first is called by the unpromising name of "Co-operative Education." A special chapter of this book is devoted to an explanation of this system and I need only mention it here as one of the most important developments in connection with education in any country in modern times. It has swept through University and School. Every one who examines it in America desires to extend it. I think its advantages are obvious in every way. It is a thoroughly democratic system also, and gives valuable training in other ways before the young student commences his life's work. He learns to get on with men of a different social class, and what has proved so helpful in its working is the kind of relation between the student from the university, and the ordinary workmen on the railway, and other concerns. It also gives him an interest in, and sympathy with, conditions of labour.

Another experiment that I would like to speak of very briefly is the establishment of what is called the "Modern School" in America. I know no country in the world where experiment is so free as in America. There is a delight in experiment—experiment sometimes for its own sake. Not all these experiments are wise, of course, but it is a great asset to the education of a country to have the spirit of experiment, and the power to carry it out.

America, of course, has what does not exist in this country, at any rate not at present, though —in view of the fortunes made during the war —it may exist soon. She has great private benefactors to the cause of education. Many wealthy men in America have done the best thing they could do with a portion of their capital, having handed over great sums for the purpose of education. One of the largest educational trusts of America is the General Education Board. A Board like that—with a duty incumbent upon it to experiment—exercises an inspiring influence over the whole position of general education. So one of the most recent

4–2

experiments in America is the founding of the modern school.

The modern school was founded under the auspices of the General Education Board. They did not commit themselves to all the details, but they were willing for the experiment to be tried. The modern school really represents a revolt against being guided only by tradition and convention in education. The modern school set out with the principle that, because a thing has been done before or practised throughout the ages, it does not mean that it is necessarily right to do it to-day. That sounds revolutionary, but that is the stage they have got to there. They declare that because a subject has been taught year after year for centuries that is no reason for investing that subject, or the methods of teaching it, with a peculiar sanctity, and placing it above criticism. That is the sort of basis upon which they approached the foundation of the modern school. They determined to work on this basis: to have no subject in the curriculum which they did not believe to be good for the child, apart from whether it had been taught before or not. Let us consider, they said, only the needs of the child. I cannot go into a great mass of details, but I will simply state that they divide the life of the child into certain divisions, such as science, civics, ethics, literature, etc., and base the curriculum on the needs of the child. They considered that, there being now a vast accumulation of fresh human knowledge, it was necessary, if only in view of this increase, to revise the curriculum, and not to neglect vast tracts of knowledge simply because there was a conventional curriculum in existence which had served for centuries. That is why they tried to proceed from interests and objects surrounding the child, working from his immediate interests to other interests far away from him, but beginning with the things around him. In science, for instance, they would not first begin with a theory, but with the things around him, such as the electric light, etc. In languages, they would have a natural bias for modern languages, and would make the child a citizen of the world. In literature, they would not take a great poem by Milton or Shakespeare, and say, "This is literature; you must, and shall like it." On the contrary, they would be delighted if the boy loved *Treasure Island*, even if he hated Chaucer, because the first thing was to get him interested in reading for its own sake, and they would work through his enthusiasm, once aroused, instead of working from standards he could not appreciate.

I am afraid I have been longer than I intended to be, and there is still a vast amount that I should like to have said. Let me close with one other great experiment before I give an opportunity for questions. I refer to an experiment which is being made with the object of encouraging corporate life and feeling, civic feeling, in the elementary and secondary schools. A common feature of the equipment in these schools is the assembly hall. For instance, in a New York secondary school you would find an assembly hall, which would not hold all the children, but perhaps one-third. At certain intervals during the day, school assemblies take place. In some schools there are four assemblies, in others they go on all day long, that is to say, a section of the school, 200, 500, or 1000 of the scholars, come together for an assembly, which may last an hour, but the length of time varies. This is made use of as a distinct exercise for the pupils in all sorts of ways, *e.g.* in the art of living together, of speaking in public, of developing individuality. For a big assembly you will find, perhaps, 1000 children walking in, without any drill or mechanical precision, but in a perfectly orderly way, and sitting in their places. If the hour of the assembly has not been reached, they will talk quietly together; but at the hour for the assembly a boy or girl chairman will start the meeting, silence being observed, and the proceedings conducted throughout with perfect

dignity and order. The minutes of the last
meeting will be read and signed, and the pro-
gramme for that particular assembly will be
gone through. Perhaps a question is debated,
or some school songs sung, or some readings
given, or original work done by the children.
Perhaps visitors are there, and the children
address the visitors, telling them about the
school, and asking the visitors to say a few words;
but the whole thing is a unique spectacle of
self-government, though carried out by so young
an audience.

I have endeavoured to cover a very wide field.
If I have praised the system greatly, I admit that
there are some things to criticise or condemn;
but in many respects America, in her splendid
system of education, offers an example to the
rest of the civilised world.

CHAPTER FOUR

THE CO-OPERATIVE SYSTEM OF EDUCATION
IN AMERICA : BY J. HOWARD WHITEHOUSE

ONE of the most important developments
in American education affects materially
both the universities and the high schools. This
is known there as the co-operative system of
education, and was first tried as an experiment
in the Colleges of Engineering of the University
of Cincinnati ten years ago. The inception of
the system is due to Professor Schneider of that
university. He made an experimental trial of
the system in the school year of 1906–7. It
has proved a remarkable success. It has been
extended to many other universities and to the
high schools in 300 American towns, and it has
caused a revolution in certain departments of
university and high school instruction.

The term "co-operative education" is used
in America to describe a new method of uniting
practical training and experience with theoretical
instruction. Before it was tried the usual method
in colleges and universities was to have school
workshops. But it is obvious that these must
always be inadequate. If they are to give
students the practical training they require, they

must include reproductions of the plants of foundries, railways and industries, and all the vast mechanism of the world of industry. Expense and space would make such an attempt an impossibility. Even if it were possible to conceive of the provision of plant on such a scale for the purpose of practical instruction in a single institution, the fact that it is constantly being changed and improved in the industrial world would soon put it out of date.

So far, therefore, as practical training is confined to the college, it must always be of a strictly limited nature. The founder of the system of co-operative education, faced with this difficulty, resolved, instead of continuing to establish "shops" within the university, to attempt to use the works and plant of the great engineering firms, the railways, and other industrial undertakings, for the purpose of practical instruction, the theoretical side of the work being reserved for the university. The scheme was tried with twenty-eight students. The course mapped out for them extended over a period of six years, alternate weeks being spent at the university and in the shops of the firms co-operating. These firms numbered twelve engineering concerns who had agreed to try the new system for a period of nine months, corresponding to the college year. The students who were willing to try the new experiment were selected with care. The test they were subjected to under the new plan was a severe one, as it entailed doing an ordinary day's work at manual labour in hot weather on equal terms with ordinary apprentices. Some of them fell out, but it was easy to fill up their places.

The students who were taking the new course did not, of course, all go into the workshops together. During any week when half were in the shops, the other half were at the university, so firms entering into the experiment had an even supply of student-labour. Roughly speaking each student had a partner; when one was in the shop the other was in the university. At the end of a year it was demonstrated that the new plan could be successfully worked; and the problem before the university was how quickly it could adapt itself in order to meet the large number of applications from students who were willing to enter the scheme for training for a great variety of industries of the most skilled character. Not only were there numerous applications from prospective students, but all hesitation on the part of employers disappeared and an ample number were willing to co-operate with the university. Obviously, however, the number of students who could be received was limited by the accommodation in the class rooms and laboratories of the university. At the end of four years the new plan had been fully vindicated; and it had been adapted to a variety of courses which included civil, chemical, and metallurgical engineering, and to a number of industries ranging from railway construction to the manufacture of ink.

The first four years were regarded as experimental and many changes in detail were made as experience was gained. It was, for instance, made easy for a student to be transferred from one kind of work to another when a change seemed desirable. A special agency was set up in the university to handle all business questions so that the members of the faculty were left free to consider educational problems proper. The six-year course appeared to be longer than was necessary, and it was reduced to five years. The scheme of weekly alternation between college and workshop was changed to a fortnightly alternation. The curriculum was also modified from time to time. When the school year of 1910–11 was reached the principal changes in the system had been made, and the experimental stage was regarded as ended. But the directors of the new plan always believed in making it adaptable. This was especially necessary in order to meet the needs of the firms who co-operated in many different industries. The scheme was therefore made flexible without being desultory and definite without being rigid. It is found possible for the co-operative course at any university to be worked in conjunction with firms within a radius of 100 miles of the university.

It may be of value to describe the system which is observed, so far as the life of the student is concerned, during the fortnight he spends in the workshops of the firm receiving him under the course arranged. Whatever the industry, the student always begins at the bottom, so that his knowledge of every phase of the business may be complete. If it is railway engineering, the least skilled work would first be his, connected, perhaps, with the laying of the track; and so in every industry. The student enters the works on the same terms as other workmen and receives the same rate of pay according to the class of work, the minimum rate for beginners being 25 cents (1s.) per hour. In America, where the highest forms of education are taken advantage of by the poor to a much greater extent than in this country, this arrangement is a great help to poor men. The university professors are responsible not only for the school work of the students, but for their workshop too. They are relieved of all business details, but they are responsible for the co-ordination of the school and shop work. Special co-ordinators, who are members of the faculty, are appointed to keep in touch with the shop work and to see that the practical work of each student is properly related to his work within the university. Each student has a work record card, and this card contains full details of the work done in the shops, the name of the firm he is working with, the number of hours worked, and all other relevant details. In addition to the personal record card, which each man retains, the university keeps a very elaborate record of every student under the system during the whole of his university course.

The system has extended from the university, which gave it birth, to many others, and it is to-day being rapidly developed in many parts of America. Even more interesting is the fact that it has spread in a modified form to the high school and, as already stated, has been adopted in one form or another in the schools of many towns. The chief industries and businesses to which it has been extended in connection with the high schools are mail order houses, department stores, machine shops, railways, automobile factories, printing offices, and electric light and power companies. The method follows, with certain modifications, the line adopted in the universities. In one high school (Fitchburg,

Mass.) the students, after spending one year wholly in school, work during alternate weeks as apprentices—machinists, pattern-makers, draughtsmen, printers, or textile workers. At other schools the industries at which the students work are determined by the industrial activities in the district. The system has been introduced into several of the high schools of New York, and co-operation is being carried on with leading commercial and manufacturing houses in or near the city.

Experiments have already taken place with the object of applying co-operative education to agriculture. They have been successful, and great developments may be seen in the near future. The experiments which have taken place affect both the high schools and the universities. It must be borne in mind that to whatever industry or profession the system is applied the object is to make the work educational; and it is of particular importance to remember this in connection with the application of the plan to agriculture. The United States Bureau of Education thus expresses itself on this point:

There is no particular cultural value in a boy milking cows, for instance, or cultivating corn, after he has done it a few times; but if he will do a certain amount of reading in connection with the work, keep records of yield and cost, and make experiments which require him to think, that is educational.

This principle is observed in the experiments which have begun in connection with agriculture. In one high school (Northampton, Mass.) during a course of four years, the students have four home tasks, each of which occupies a year. They receive credit for each of these tasks which is satisfactorily done (*i.e.* they count towards the work required for a certificate of graduation). If the student elects to cultivate an acre of ground the first year, he will receive credit for the work if he carries out the instructions which are given to him. The next year he may decide to take charge of two, four, or six cows according to his age. He must do all the work himself and keep detailed records in order to secure credit for the work at school. This plan has already proved its success and has been helpful both to the school and to the community.

CHAPTER FIVE

SOME SUGGESTIONS FOR THE PROMOTION
OF INTERNATIONAL EDUCATION : BY
J. HOWARD WHITEHOUSE

I T is now a commonplace of every tongue that war is an evil, and that the hope of the world is in its elimination. But the consummation which all desire is not yet. It may be hastened by wiser methods of education based upon the recognition of the fact that our youth have now to be citizens of the world, and to be prepared for international as well as national duties.

The League of Nations may become a mere piece of official machinery, as useless as the old diplomacy to prevent war. It may, on the other hand, become an effective instrument for world co-operation and peace. But to do this it must have behind it the knowledge, enthusiasms and conscious ideals of Peoples. For these we must ultimately rely in a large measure upon the schools of this and other countries.

The first suggestion I would make in attempting to build up a system of international education is that we should adopt different methods of teaching history in our schools. We all know what the ordinary school text-books were like which were in use before the war. English History stood out for the most part as a succession of military events. Our heroes were the fighting heroes. Even some histories with literary pretensions were disfigured by a narrow and flamboyant nationalistic appeal.

The limited picture given in most school histories rarely extended far beyond our own country. There was little attempt to give any sort of international teaching of history. In schools where real historical work is being done, it has been frequently found necessary to dispense with text-books, and to encourage pupils to make these for themselves by the writing of their own notes.

The history of our own country should be taught in relation to the history of other countries. Our conscious ideal should be to bring not only knowledge but sympathy and understanding for the help of the youth of our schools. For it is only through a reformed method of the teaching of history that we can hope to give the right bias to the young student in his outlook on foreign affairs.

It sounds a commonplace to say that the teachers of history must themselves have a definite ideal of the interdependence of mankind and nations, of their solidarity. Frequently we have hesitated to express that ideal with all its implications. Its expression was never more necessary than it is now. We have emerged from a war which all over the world has increased passion, and prejudice and narrow nationalist feelings. Our hope is in the schools. There we must ultimately look for the broadening of sympathy and the understanding of the lessons of the past which may yet lead peoples into the paths of peace and freedom. There are few signs yet that the world has learnt these lessons. We are invited to rejoice at the death of the devil; it may be we are bidden to his resurrection feast.

We have not yet secured in our schools freedom for ideals. Let us get rid of the drill sergeant in education.

A few years ago, at a famous public school, an attempt was made by reasonable masters interested in real things, to guide—I think in a wise and intelligent way—the sympathies of their pupils. These masters interested them in the study of contemporary history and events, and the result of that experiment was to stir up an amount of interest and enthusiasm in real things which had an extraordinary influence for good in the whole life of the school, as well as in the individual lives of the pupils who took up these studies. It is within my knowledge that the War Office intervened, and pointed out to

the authorities of the school that if liberal
studies like that were continued and boys were
encouraged to think for themselves on such
questions, they feared that it would have a
prejudicial influence upon the work of the
Officers' Training Corps. They therefore warned
the authorities of the school that they would have
to withdraw their support of the school as one
where the O.T.C. was officially recognised, if
this scheme continued. I am sorry to say that
as a result of that intervention, the authorities
of the school suppressed this teaching and dis-
missed the brilliant men responsible for its
inception. That is why I say we must be
delivered from the drill sergeant in education.

One great obstacle to international education
is the fact that most people are wholly dependent
upon the newspaper press for all foreign news
and views. It is an inadequate and frequently
a biased agency. It has always seemed to me
lamentable that, with few exceptions, it is
impossible to get any coherent picture of the
lives of peoples in other countries. If we think
of almost any newspaper, the columns devoted
to foreign affairs consist largely of unrelated
telegrams having reference to dramatic events
—crimes, prize-fights, or anything that momen-
tarily interests the general public. We seek in
vain for the newspaper which will supply from

the great capitals of the world a coherent story from day to day giving a picture of the life and interests, the literature, the social problems, of the peoples of the modern world. I do not want to know how the champion eater is faring in New York; I am not greatly concerned with the sensational crimes of Paris, or the latest creation of her milliners; but I do want to know what ordinary people are thinking and reading and trying to do, the development of their social structure, their attitude towards other countries. These things are sought in vain. There is a great, and in some respects an unexplored, avenue of international service before the English newspaper which is prepared to recognise its responsibilities and opportunities as an instrument of international education.

Perhaps the best of all ways to promote friendship between peoples is for the people of one nation personally to know the people of another nation, but this always appears to me the most difficult thing to achieve. I am sure that it is not sufficient for us to be content with the exchange of official representatives, whether ambassadors, bishops, or business men. Notwithstanding the respect I feel for all persons in authority, I sometimes think that when they speak in the name of their fellow-countrymen, they are not wholly adequate.

I have read and heard many speeches by distinguished people abroad, especially in America, made in the name of this country, which are foolish and mischievous. Even an interchange of churches which is so much talked of, where ministers of all denominations are sent to this country and are balanced by a selected number of ministers sent to another country, though the results may be good if all tribal gods are left behind, is not adequate if we are going to seek for real knowledge and friendship between the peoples of the world. I have no quick solution to offer. I believe profoundly in the extraordinary good that comes from individual travel, but it is impossible to suggest that the whole of the people of the nation should be sent on foreign tours. Yet I earnestly plead that we should have far more international travel between students than has existed hitherto. Let them go themselves as far as possible, and live amongst other people, and know something about other schools and universities and ways; let them go with sympathy and understanding, with the desire to learn, with the feeling that their own country is one country in the brotherhood of nations. I believe that every person who comes under those broadening spiritual impulses will in himself be a centre for spreading the lessons he has learnt.

In the past, the peoples of the world have had no real share in the problems that their rulers have solved for them—or have failed to solve. Their part has been to pay the penalty for the sins of others. The only way in which Governments can be controlled in their international relationships is through popular knowledge united with ideals. A country having ideals, and the power to give effect to them, will not long tolerate the old diplomatists. We shall see no change in the animosities between peoples and rulers, nor any real advance made by such schemes as the League of Nations, unless we have in every country a spiritually educated democracy. It is the duty of the schools to give this spiritual education. As such education becomes world-wide, one of the greatest obstacles to progress will have been removed, the fact that, even among the greatest nations to-day, vitally different standards of life and thought exist.

SOME PRACTICAL EXPERIMENTS

Having dealt so far with the general question of international education, I turn to the consideration of some practical experiments which are being carried out at a public school, in the hope that they may prove suggestive or helpful

to all who are interested in education. The school
is the new public school founded at Bembridge
upon the Council of which the Society for
Experiment and Research in Education is
represented. The school aims to give all its
members who have reached a certain age definite
international teaching with the object of pro-
moting the knowledge and understanding of
the history and peoples of other countries. The
experiments in question are based upon the
belief that if the world is to be mended, the
coming generation must be taught that civilisation is a collective achievement and a common
responsibility, and that an intelligent knowledge
of other countries and other peoples is an
essential part of the equipment of the modern
citizen.

It is attempted to achieve the objects in view
by a variety of methods, which include the
following:

1. Civics. It is sought to arouse and extend
interest in foreign questions by encouraging it
in local and national matters. The older boys
all pass through a course of study in civics, and
a special section of the library is provided for their
use. Local and national forms and problems of
Government are considered. The work is co-
ordinated with the teaching of modern history.
The boys are, of course, protected against

doctrinaire or party teaching. It is sought to strengthen in the boys the impulse towards unselfish work for the good of others. Excursions at home and abroad help to make the subject real.

2. The Teaching of History. English history is not taught as an unrelated subject but side by side with the modern history of Europe and America. Older boys are given a clear outline of the development of the nations of Europe and America, and the chief problems confronting them to-day. National and International questions, such as the League of Nations, and others arising out of the war, are studied. Essays are written, papers are read, and discussions held.

The authorities of the school are face to face with the difficulty that confronts all who wish to reform the teaching of modern history, that is, the absence of adequate text-books. Mr Wells, in his *Outline History of the World*, has done a great service to the cause of international education, for his book constitutes a unique attempt to present the study of history as a united whole. His work makes, within certain limits, a first class book of reference for older boys. The method is being tried of encouraging boys to make their own text-books by the careful writing up of their own lecture notes. Such a method is only possible with older boys and then only to a limited degree.

3. A School International Committee. It is, however, sought to make the individual boy interested in a personal sense in the peoples of other countries. For this purpose the boys elect a School International Committee consisting of four or five members. This Committee acts for the whole school, and among other things they attempt the following: correspondence with representative schools in other countries and exchange of school publications; the maintenance of an international notice board upon which each day cuttings are displayed relating to interesting events in other countries; they collect illustrations of current events and topical subjects appearing abroad, and display these in the school, and they arrange for foreign newspapers and magazines. They also arrange for lectures on subjects affecting other lands, either from inside the school, or from outside.

4. The study of Contemporary Events. An even more important way in which personal interest is aroused is perhaps the regular study of contemporary events. Each week the story of events in the chief places of the world is told. It is related as a coherent story. The boys write up weekly a narrative from their notes taken during the lectures. The result of these methods is shown in the use which is made of the newspapers in their newspaper room. They are read

day by day, not only for their athletic news, but with a real interest in the great drama of world events. Advantage is taken of the periods devoted to this study of contemporary events to interest the boys in many aspects of life and thought in other lands. The present is linked with the past. Important events are traced as far as possible to their source. The lives of great persons are briefly studied. The progress of science and invention in other countries is watched. Maps and other illustrations are used whenever practicable. An examination is held at the end of each term.

Again, such a question as of the League of Nations is not studied as a mere academic matter, or as a piece of machinery, or even as represented by its official supporters. The boys try to see for themselves how it should or could affect definite questions. Thus they review such a question as the relations say, between Italy and Greece and after trying to understand the facts consider the possibilities of dealing with it through the League of Nations. No doubt they wish to travel more quickly than the League. No doubt their suggestions are often crude and impracticable; but the results are wholly good. Many of the boys have realised the joy of thinking about real things and have found new intellectual interests which show themselves in a variety of ways. Thus they developed a scheme for offering hospitality to two boys from the famine area of Europe, and by their own work they raised a not inconsiderable sum of money for their young guests.

5. Another expression of their intellectual interest was seen in the formation of a Society for the study of Local History. A number of the members of this society have produced a book upon the country round about them. One boy deals with its records in modern history; another with its Roman associations; another with its literary associations. Others write upon its bird life, its agriculture, its trees, flowers and insects. Other sections deal with the history of its old buildings, the wonders of its seashore, and the geology of its cliffs. It is found in practice that the boy who is keen on local history, is keen also upon international history. Perhaps, too, the reverse is equally true. The two subjects appear interdependent and equally helpful the one to the other as sources of inspiration.

The book is published and submitted to the judgment of its readers, not as a finished piece of scholarship, or of literature, but as the expression of the genuine enthusiasm felt by the authors of the book in real things, and as a record of a co-operative adventure voluntarily undertaken.

6. Visits are made to foreign countries. These visits were not possible during the War, but

are now being re-organised. Each year the
boys spend a week or two in a foreign country;
the history, language and architecture of the
places to be visited are studied before each
journey and a specially prepared booklet is
issued, giving historical, literary, architectural
and other details with maps. Similar visits take
place in England. In this connection, it may
be pointed out that no teaching of a modern
language is justified unless it enables the pupils
to become proficient in that language and to use
it as a means of communication. It is the aim
of the school to give each boy a mastery of
French, and this object is greatly helped by the
foreign journeys.

7. The school and America. Special em-
phasis is laid upon the teaching of American
history, and the study of current events there.
This is done with the deliberate intention of
cultivating the closest feelings of friendship
and admiration for that country. It is, in many
ways, the best country with which to begin
experiments in international education, for there
is here no language difficulty. The course of
study includes the general outlines of the history
of America with a specialised study of its great
epochs and its great men, and I think it would
be fair to say that there is a resultant feeling of
interest and good will which will lead many boys
in later years to visit America, and will give all

of them a desire permanently to work for the close friendship of the two nations. A scheme is under consideration by which one or two members of the staff will be enabled to visit America from time to time and cultivate personal relationships with schools there.

8. The study of history has been made more real by debates upon great questions. These are prepared for by individual research. Thus, one form has recently discussed the question of the American Civil War. Almost all the boys in the form took part. Each was given a separate aspect of the subject to read up and to speak upon. A vote is usually taken at the end of these discussions.

9. The school library is an indispensable aid to international education. It has been found helpful to have reading periods in school hours for most forms and to use these opportunities for interesting boys in historical novels, biographical studies, and similar books which would help to give them a broad outlook on to the affairs of the world.

10. A few other methods used in the school may be briefly summarised. I have spoken of the need for better methods of historical teaching in order that boys should understand other countries and their people. They should also be taught that knowledge and thought are international. They are led to realise this by

the appreciation of the literature, art, music, and other achievements by the people of other countries. Each week there is a musical recital, which includes work by representative musicians of foreign countries. The school has a special museum and art gallery which is used for temporary exhibitions. A different subject is illustrated each term by a special exhibition, and these sometimes relate to the art and life of other countries. Historical research prizes have been instituted and these deal, too, with international subjects in the broadest sense. The interest of boys in original research work has been greatly helped by the recent publication in book form of the best of their essays. Some of these are an expression of their international interests. We have been able to welcome at the school visitors from other countries, including great travellers and statesmen.

The result of these and other methods has been, I think, to promote a more tolerant and thoughtful outlook on the world of to-day on the part of the senior boys of the school. These studies and interests have also helped to develop their own personality, and to prepare them for the work which must fall upon the youth of the world.

For EU product safety concerns, contact us at Calle de José Abascal, 56–1°, 28003 Madrid, Spain or eugpsr@cambridge.org.

www.ingramcontent.com/pod-product-compliance
Ingram Content Group UK Ltd.
Pitfield, Milton Keynes, MK11 3LW, UK
UKHW012334130625
459647UK00009B/270